ISBN 978-1-332-59662-1
PIBN 10001043

This book is a reproduction of an important historical work. Forgotten Books uses state-of-the-art technology to digitally reconstruct the work, preserving the original format whilst repairing imperfections present in the aged copy. In rare cases, an imperfection in the original, such as a blemish or missing page, may be replicated in our edition. We do, however, repair the vast majority of imperfections successfully; any imperfections that remain are intentionally left to preserve the state of such historical works.

1 MONTH OF
FREE
READING

at
www.ForgottenBooks.com

By purchasing this book you are eligible for one month membership to ForgottenBooks.com, giving you unlimited access to our entire collection of over 1,000,000 titles via our web site and mobile apps.

To claim your free month visit:
www.forgottenbooks.com/free1043

Fundamental Principles

of the

Baconian Ciphers

Franciscus Bacon,
Ætatis suæ 18.
1578.

AND APPLICATION TO BOOKS OF THE
SIXTEENTH AND SEVENTEENTH CENTURIES

Compiled by George Fabyan

In Homage to the Memory of

Isabella Francis Fabyan

Her Boy

dedicates this work which he considers his best

to Mother

Foreword

In certain volumes published in the 16th and 17th centuries, the use and commixture, without any apparent reason, of two forms of type, both in the roman and the italic letters, has long been a matter of comment and discussion among lovers of books and book lore, and although various theories have been advanced by researchers and students of Elizabethan literature, none of them have seemed to answer the question.

Twenty years ago, Elizabeth Wells Gallup, an instructor in English, was reading an original of Sir Francis Bacon's *De Augmentis Scientiarum* and the chapter on Ciphers appealed strongly to her reason. Of the books of the Elizabethan period, none are of greater importance than the 1623 Shakespeare Folio, which contains a vast number of examples of the use of two forms of type. She asked herself whether there might not be concealed within this work a cipher such as Bacon described.

Bacon explains in the above mentioned chapter how a secret or interior note may be infolded within an apparently simple open or exterior message by the use of two forms of type very similar in appearance but still showing to the closely observant or experienced eye distinct characteristics, by means of which these two forms may be distinguished. Bacon calls attention to the mathematical fact that the transposition of only two different objects (blocks, letters, etc.) will yield thirty-two dissimilar combinations, of which only twenty-four would be necessary to represent all the letters of our alphabet (I and J, U and V, being used interchangeably in the 16th century). By referring to the code given by Bacon it will readily be seen that a row of fifteen blocks in which the 1st, 4th, 8th, 9th, 10th, and 13th were black, the rest white, would spell out the word "the". If black and white blocks are replaced by capital and small letters respectively, the name

BilterAL CipHer

still contains the hidden word "the". But now suppose the differences between the two forms (called for convenience the *a* and the *b* forms) are not so apparent as in the above examples; suppose that in this name "Bi-literal Cipher," letters of two only very slightly different, but still distinguishable, forms were used, it is clear that the word "the" could still be infolded within it. Hence by the appropriate use of type of two forms, a sentence, a paragraph, a page or an entire book, might be made to infold a hidden message of an import wholly different from the apparent language of the printed page. Nor is this *reading between* the lines, but it is *discovering in* the lines something not apparent at a cursory glance. Neither is it necessary in order to achieve this that the original language of the printed page be framed, altered, or modified for the purpose in any manner whatsoever. It is only necessary that after the obvious or open language of the manuscript is written, some distinguishing mark should be placed, for the direction of the printer, under each letter which is to be set up from the *b* form. All the other letters would naturally be set up from the *a* form.

To decipher such material then, it would be necessary first to be able to recognize the *a* and the *b* forms in the type used, and secondly, to know the code which had been employed.

Having mastered the examples given by Lord Bacon in both the editions of *De Augmentis Scientiarum* or "The Advancement of Learning," Mrs. Gallup determined to apply the principles of Bacon's Bi-literal Cipher to the 1623 Shakespeare Folio. Opening the Folio at random she turned the leaves to select the page of the most characteristic italic type she could find, and chose the page containing the Prologue to "Troilus and Cressida", in which even a casual inspection will disclose the presence of two forms of type for certain letters. (Note such outstanding examples as the capital *I's,* the capital *N's,* the capital *T's,* and the small *w's.*) Having noticed the undoubted presence of two forms of type, Mrs. Gallup's first step in endeavoring to determine whether this page does or does not contain the Bi-literal Cipher, was to study the differences between these two forms; her next step was to decide which was to be termed the *a* form and which the *b* form. The fact that in Bacon's code the *a's* predominate greatly over the *b's,* suggested to Mrs. Gallup that the *a* form might probably be that occurring most frequently on the printed page, *if the code given by Bacon had actually been used.* Examining each letter under a magnifying glass, she tentatively assigned each one as an *a* or a *b* form, marking it accordingly. Having completed the marking in this manner, she applied Bacon's own code but without any intelligible result. She noticed, however, near the bottom of the page, that the groups of *a* and *b* resulted in giving by application of the Code a collection of letters as follows:

ELIZXBEXH

(X:—Mrs. Gallup does not remember the two letters where *X* is used in the above word.)

She realized that this combination of letters was probably intended to spell out the word "Elizabeth." She changed carefully the markings of the groups which formed the letters here designated by *X*, making, as she did so, sketches of the characteristics and differences of the letters she so changed in producing the word "Elizabeth." Then with this additional information, Mrs. Gallup carefully marked each letter of the Prologue anew—to find to her own amazement, when she had finished, the astounding message which the student will himself have the pleasure of deciphering in a succeeding lesson. After the Prologue, she studied and deciphered other passages concealed in the apparently meaningless type forms. Later she applied the methods to a number of 16th and 17th century works, with negative results in certain cases, but positive results in others.

Such, then, is the history of the discovery of the use of a cryptic or secret writing in certain of the aforementioned volumes, which for three hundred years escaped detection—The Bi-literal Cipher of Sir Francis Bacon.

The advantages to be gained from the study of the Bi-literal Cipher are many and various:—it calls into play both literary knowledge and technical and mechanical skill; it trains the eye to close observance; it trains the hands in printing, which is now almost a lost art; it requires and teaches not only accuracy, but the absolute necessity for accuracy, which is very desirable in any walk of life—in a word, the study of the Cipher may, when pursued earnestly and accurately, achieve that most-to-be-desired end of all education, a thoroughly trained mind. As for its historic value, that is inestimable, as the search after Truth is the greatest of all pursuits. In addition, its practical values are numerous: it may be utilized in kindergarten teaching in blocks, beads, weaving, or colors; in the entertainment and education of children, old people, or invalids, it may be an easy and most pleasant factor; and in the instruction of the blind, the use of the cipher embossed and placed vertically would require the learning of but *two* differences or characters in place of *twenty-six;* and finally, let it not be forgotten that the Cipher permits of transmission of thought, regardless of censorship or the curiosity of others.

The mastering of the principles of the Bi-literal Cipher is really a simple matter. Young people of fourteen years and upwards, it is found, note readily differences in type. One young student in the Riverbank Laboratories marked 940 letters in three hours with only eight errors. But the application of these principles to the Elizabethan volumes which contain the Bi-literal Cipher is a more difficult matter; first, because in order to escape suspicion and detection at a premature time, and secondly, because of the unavoidable variation due to the imperfect methods of printing in use at that time, the two forms of type are not so clearly distinguishable as in the examples given by Bacon himself. However, the earnest student will in time overcome these obstacles, and by concentrated application learn to decipher even the most difficult passages and works. After all possible mechanical assistance has been provided, the requisites on the part of the student are only earnest purpose, good eyes, and a good mind.

speak of stories or metre) it is (as I said before) like a luxuriant plant, that comes of the lust of the earth, without any formal seed. Wherefore it spreads everywhere and is scattered far and wide,—so that it would be vain to take thought about the defects of it. With this therefore we need not trouble our-selves. And with regard to Accents of words, it is too small a matter to speak of; unless perhaps it be thought worth remaik-ing, that while the accentuation of *words* has been exquisitely observed, the accentuation of *sentences* has not been observed at all And yet it is common to all mankind almost to drop-the voice at the end of a period, to raise it in asking a question, and other things of the kind not a few. And so much for the part of Grammar which relates to Speech.

As for Writing, it is performed either by the common al-phabet (which is used by everybody) or by a secret and pri-vate one, agreed upon by particular persons; which they call *ciphers.* And with regard to the common orthography itself, a controversy and question has been raised among us,—namely, whether words ought to be written as they are pronounced, or in the usual way. But this apparently reformed style of writing (viz. in which the spelling should agree with the pronuncia-tion) belongs to the class of unprofitable subtleties. For the pronunciation itself is continually changing; it does not remain fixed; and the derivations of words, especially from foreign tongues, are thereby completely obscured. And as the spelling of words according to the fashion is no check at all upon the fashion of pronunciation, but leaves it free, to what purpose is this innovation?

Let us proceed then to Ciphers. Of these there are many kinds: simple ciphers; ciphers mixed with non-significant characters; ciphers containing two different letters in one character; wheel-ciphers; key-ciphers; word-ciphers; and the like. But the virtues required in them are three; that they be easy and not laborious to write; that they be safe, and impossible to be deciphered; and lastly that they be, if possible, such as not to raise suspicion. For if letters fall into the hands of those who have power either over the writers or over those to whom they are addressed, although the cipher itself may be safe and impossible to decipher, yet the matter comes under examination and question; unless the cipher be such as either to raise no suspicion or to elude inquiry. Now for this

elusion of inquiry, there is a new and useful contrivance for it, which as I have it by me, why should I set it down among the desiderata, instead of propounding the thing itself? It is this: let a man have two alphabets, one of true letters, the other of non-significants; and let him infold in them two letters at once; one carrying the secret, the other such a letter as the writer would have been likely to send, and yet without anything dangerous. Then if any one be strictly examined as to the cipher, let him offer the alphabet of non significants for the true letters, and the alphabet of true letters for non-significants. Thus the examiner will fall upon the exterior letter; which finding probable, he will not suspect anything of another letter within. But for avoiding suspicion altogether, I will add another contrivance, which I devised myself when I was at Paris in my early youth, and which I still think worthy of preservation. For it has the perfection of a cipher, which is to make anything signify anything; subject however to this condition, that the infolding writing shall contain at least five times as many letters as the writing infolded: no other condi-tion or restriction whatever is required. The way to do it is this: First let all the letters of the alphabet be resolved into transpositions of two letters only. For the transposition of two letters through five places will yield thirty-two differences; much more twenty-four, which is the number of letters in our alphabet. Here is an example of such an alphabet.

Example of an Alphabet in two letters.

A	B	C	D	E	F	G
Aaaaa.	aaaab.	aaaba.	aaabb.	aabaa.	aabab.	aabba.
H	I	K	L	M	N	O
aabbb.	abaaa.	abaab.	ababa.	ababb.	abbaa.	abbab.
P	Q	R	S	T	V	W
abbba.	abbbb.	baaaa.	baaab.	baaba.	baabb.	babaa.
X	Y	Z.				
babab.	babba.	babbb.				

Nor is it a slight thing which is thus by the way effected. For hence we see how thoughts may be communicated at any distance of place by means of any objects perceptible either to the eye or ear, provided only that those objects are capable of two differences; as by bells, trumpets, torches, gunshots, and the like. But to proceed with our business: when you prepare to write, you must reduce the interior epistle to this biliteral alphabet. Let the interior epistle be

Fly.

Example of reduction.

F   L   Y.
aabab.   ababa.   babba.

Have by you at the same time another alphabet in two forms; I mean one in which each of the letters of the common alphabet, both capital and small, is exhibited in two different forms,—any forms that you find convenient.

Example of an Alphabet in two forms.

a	b	a	b	a	b	a	b	a	b	a	b
A	A	a	a	B	B	b	b	C	C	c	c
D	D	d	d	E	E	e	e	F	F	f	f
G	G	g	g	H	H	h	h	I	I	i	i
K	K	k	k	L	L	l	l	M	M	m	m
N	N	n	n	O	O	o	o	P	P	p	p
Q	Q	q	q	R	R	r	r	S	S	s	s
T	T	t	t	U	U	u	u	V	V	v	v
W	W	w	w	X	X	x	x	Y	Y	y	y

Then take your interior epistle, reduced to the biliteral shape, and adapt to it letter by letter your exterior epistle in the biform character; and then write it out. Let the exterior epistle be,

Do not go till I come.

Example of Adaptation.

F   L   Y.
aa bab.   ab aba.b   a bba.
Do not go   till   I   come.

I add another larger example of the same cipher,—of the writing of any thing by anything.

The interior epistle; for which I have selected the Spartan despatch, formerly sent in the *Scytale.*

All is lost. Mindarus is killed. The soldiers want food. We can neither get hence, nor stay longer here.

The exterior epistle, taken from Cicero's first letter, and containing the Spartan despatch within it.

In all duty or rather piety towards you I satisfy every body except myself. Myself I never satisfy. For so great are the services which you have rendered me, that seeing you did not rest in your endeavours on my behalf till the thing was done, I feel as if life had lost all its sweetness, because I cannot do as much in this cause of yours. The occasions are these: Ammonius the King's ambassador openly besieges us with money: the business is carried on through the same creditors who were employed in it when you were here, &c.

The doctrine of Ciphers carries along with it another doctrine, which is its relative. This is the doctrine of deciphering, or of detecting ciphers, though one be quite ignorant of the alphabet used or the private understanding between the parties: a thing requiring both labour and ingenuity, and dedicated, as the other likewise is, to the secrets of princes. By skilful precaution indeed it may be made useless; though as things are it is of very great use. For if good and safe ciphers were introduced, there are very many of them which altogether elude and exclude the decipherer, and yet are sufficiently convenient and ready to read and write. But such is the rawness and unskilfulness of secretaries and clerks in the courts of kings, that the greatest matters are commonly trusted to weak and futile ciphers.

It may be suspected perhaps that in this enumeration and *census,* as I may call it, of arts, my object is to swell the ranks of the sciences thus drawn up on parade, that the numbers of them may raise admiration; whereas in so short a treatise, though the numbers may perhaps be displayed, the force and value of them can hardly be explained. But I am true to my design, and in framing this globe of knowledge I do not choose to omit even the smaller and more remote islands. And though my handling of these things be cursory, it is not (as I think) superficial; but out of a large mass of matter I pick out with a fine point the kernels and marrows of them. Of this however I leave those to judge who are most skilful in such arts. For whereas most of those who desire to be thought multiscient are given to parade the terms and externals of arts, thereby making themselves the admiration of those who do not understand those arts and the scorn of those who do; I hope that my labours will have the contrary fate, and arrest the judgment

LORD BACON'S OWN EXAMPLE OF BI-LITERAL CIPHER
Spedding's Editions 1857

Manere te volo donec venero.

Ego omni efficio ac potius pietate erga te caeteris satisfacio omnibus :
Mihi ipse nunquam satisfacio. Tanta est enim magnitudo tuorum erga
me meritorum, ut quoniam tu, nisi perfecta re, de me non conquiesti :
ego, quia non idem in tua causa efficio, vitam mihi esse acerbam putem.
In causa hæc sunt : Ammonius regis legatus aperte pecunia nos op-
pugnat : res agitur per eosdem creditores per quos cum tu aderas agebat-
tur : regis causa si qui sunt qui velint, qui pauci sunt, omnes ad Pom-
peium rem deferri volunt : senatus religionis calumniam, non religione
sed malevolentia, et illius regiae largitionis invidia comprobat, &c.

Do not go till I come.

In all duty or rather piety towards you J satisfy every body except
myself. Myself I never satisfy. For so great are the services which
you have rendered me, that seeing you did not rest in your endeavours
on my behalf till the thing was done, I feel as if life had lost all its
sweetness, because I cannot do as much in this cause of yours. The
occasions are these : Ammonius the King's ambassador openly besieges
us with money : the business is carried on through the same creditors
who were employed in it when you were here, &c.

a	b	a	b	a	b	a	b	a	b	a	b
A	D	a	d	B	E	b	e	C	F	c	f
D	G	d	g	E	H	e	h	F	I	f	i
G	K	g	k	H	L	h	l	I	M	i	m
K	N	k	n	L	O	l	o	M	P	m	p
N	Q	n	q	O	R	o	r	P	S	p	s
Q	T	q	t	R	U	r	u	S	v	s	v
T	W	t	w	U	X	u	x	v	Y	v	y
				X	Z	x	z	Y			
				Z		z					

LORD BACON'S OWN EXAMPLE OF
BI-LITERAL CIPHER

Spedding's Editions 1857

Maner etevo lodon ecven ero

Egoom nioff icioa cpoti uspie tatee rgate caete rissa
tisfa cioom nibus Mihii psenu nquam satis facio Tanta
esten immag nitud otuor umerg ameme ritor umutq uonia
mtuni siper fecta redem enonc onqui estie goqui anoni
demin tuaca usaef ficio vitam mihie sseac erbam putem
Incau sahae csunt Ammon iusre gisle gatus apert epecu
niano soppu gnatr esagi turpe reosd emcre ditor esper
quosc umtua deras ageba turre gisca usasi quisu ntqui
velin tquip aucis untom nesad Pompe iumre mdefe rrivo
lunts enatu sreli gioni scalu mniam nonre ligio nesed
malev olent iaeti llius regia elarg ition isinv idiac
ompro bat&c

Donot gotil lIcom e

Inall dutyo rrath erpie tytow ardsy ouJsa tisfy every
bodye xcept misel fMyse lfIne versa tisfy Forso great
areth eserv icesw hichy ouhav erend eredm ethat seein
gyoud idnot resti nyour endea vours onmyb ehalf tillt
hethi ngwas doneI feela sifli fehad losta llits sweet
nessb ecaus eIcan notdo asmuc hinth iscau seofy oursT
heocc asion saret heseA mmoni usthe Kings ambas sador
openl ybesi egesu swith money thebu sines sisca rried
onthr ought hesam ecred itors whowe reemp loyed initw
henyo uwere here& c

57. ITALIC TYPE-LETTERS.

The foregoing illustration of alphabets is presented at this point for the purpose of showing the differences in forms of letters resorted to in the sixteenth century (1577).

The following statement has been deciphered from Bacon's "De Augmentis" (1624) by means of the Bi-literal Cipher, " By slight alteration of the common italic letters, the alphabets of the Bi-literal Cipher, having the two forms, are readily obtained."

The "I. M. Poem" Group

The following group of illustrations has been assembled for the purpose of demonstrating the use of two forms of type in infolding a hidden message in the printed page. This series consists of various photographic facsimiles of the "I. M. Poem."—see a brief adulatory poem inserted in the preliminary pages of the 1623 Folio edition of Shakespeare's works. Although another poem—by L. Digges—appears on the same page in the original, the "I. M. Poem" has been taken as the basis of the illustration of the cipher, not because it lends itself any more easily to the purpose, but because of its brevity as compared to other passages. The message infolded in the poem is complete in itself, and is signed by its author. The illustrations are photographic copies taken from the 1623 Folio in the Newberry Library, Chicago.

The first illustration in the group is page 14, containing the photographic reproduction of the "I. M. Poem" itself, with the Student Sheet below for the convenience of those desiring to mark the letters for their own satisfaction. On page 15 opposite, are given the alphabets of the "a" and "b" forms in use in the "I. M. Poem." In these alphabets the a forms are left blank, the b forms are designated by a stroke beneath the letter. Many of these may have "variants," but a comparison of them with the typical letter of the form to which they belong makes these variations easily distinguished and understood.

> At this point the reader will turn to page 39 and open the double-hinged page showing the facsimile, the marked copy, transcription, and code, in order that it may be in view while studying the different illustrations of the poem.

The next three illustrations of the series, pages 16, 17, and 18, present photographic copies of the "I. M. Poem" with the lines so spaced as to permit of the typical form of the letter (illustrated in the alphabets on page 15) being placed over each letter of the poem. For the purpose of clearness this has been done over every third letter, and three pages therefore have been required to complete this. These pages, showing the typical form of the letter of the corresponding class a or b, facilitate the comparison between the characteristics inherent in the two forms. ·

The three pages following, pages 19, 20, and 21, show the typical letters of the opposite form to that over which each is placed. This is done for the purpose of contrast, to enable the student easily to note the differences between the two forms.

On page 22 all the letters of the "I. M. Poem" have been classified according to their respective forms in alphabetical sequence and, in the order of their respective occurrence in the text.

Page 23 of this group presents all the letters of the poem in alphabetical sequence and in the exact order of their occurrence, irrespective of the form to which they belong.

The illustration on page 39 (the hinged page) presents a copy of the "I. M. Poem" with its letters marked to show to which form each belongs, in accordance with the preceding pages. To facilitate the reading of the decipherment resulting from such marking, the letters of the poem have finally been divided into groups of five, with the result that each of such groups represents one of the combinations of *a* and *b* to be found in the Baconian Cipher Code given on the same page.

On page 24 is given additional evidence of the Cipher in the "I. M. Poem," by showing the test which was prepared by the Hon. James Phinney Baxter for Elizabeth Wells Gallup, the discoverer of the Bi-literal Cipher. Here Mr. Baxter used the exact type forms utilized in the original "I. M. Poem," but rearranged them in such a way as to incorporate a different secret message. Mrs. Gallup found the Baxter message with no less ease than the original one, both of which are given on this page for the purpose of comparison.

Beginning with page 28 will be found full descriptions of the characteristics of each typical letter of both forms. The student is recommended to refer to these descriptions as a means of familiarizing himself with the alphabets and the type forms illustrated in the preceding pages.

To the memorie of M. *W. Shake-speare*.

VVEE wondred (Shake-speare) that thou went'st so soone
  From the Worlds-Stage, to the Graues-Tyring-roome.
Wee thought thee dead, but this thy printed worth,
Tels thy Spectators, that thou went'st but forth
To enter with applause. An Actors Art,
Can dye, and liue, to acte a second part.
That's but an Exit of Mortalitie;
This, a Re-entrance to a Plaudite.

I. M.

I. M. POEM

Shakespeare Folio 1623

Tothe memor ieofM WShak espea reWEE wondr edSha kespe

areth attho uwent stsos ooneF romth eWorl dsSta getot heGra

uesTy ringr oomeW eetho ughtt heede adbut thist hypri ntedw

orthT elsth ySpec tator sthat thouw entst butfo rthTo enter

witha pplau seAnA ctors ArtCa ndyea ndliu etoac tease condp

artTh atsbu tanEx itofM ortal itieT hisaR eentr ancet oaPla

udite IM

"I.M." POEM.

VV

M   TT ee f hh ii mm oo rr tt

F SS aa ee hh ii kk pp rr ſſ tt x

SS WW aa ee hh k p rr ſſ

AA CC EE FF GG MM PP RR SS TT WW

aa bb cc dd ee ff gg hh ii ll mm nn

oo pp rr ss ſſ tt uu ww yy

ʄʄ ʄʄ is is is ſ̣ſ̣ſ̣ſ̣

— THE ALPHABETS. —

"I.M." POEM.

T h e r o *W.* a *f* a

To the memorie of M. *W.* Shake-*f*peare.

VV *w dd a fa t t o ß fn*

VV E E *wondred (Shake-fpeare) that thou went ft fo foone*

n t W l S g o e a s n g o.

From the Worlds-Stage, to the Graues-Tyring-roome.

W t y t e e b t t p n d n

Wee thought thee dead, but this thy printed worth,

T's y e t's a b m t u a b

Tels thy Spectators, that thou went ß but forth

e e i a l f n a A

To enter with applaufe. An Actors Art,

C d a l e a a a d n

Can dye, and liue, to acte a fecond part.

b s t E t M t i e

That's but an Exit of Mortalitie;

is e t n t P

This, a Re-entrance to a Plaudite. I. M.

Nº 1· COMPARISON WITH TYPICAL LETTER OF SAME FORM.

"I.M." POEM.

o e m i f   S. k p r

To the memorie of M. W. Shake-speare.

E   a r   S k p r h t u n   f o e
VVEE wondred (Shake-speare) that thou went ʃt ʃo ʃoone

a h   ʒ d t e t   G u T i r m
From the Worlds-Stage, to the Graues-Tyring-roome.

e h g t e a   u h   h r t v t
Wee thought thee dead, but this thy printed worth,

e t S ʒ t t ʒ e ʃt t r
Tels thy Spectators, that thou went ʃt but forth

T n r t p a e   A r r
To enter with applauʃe. An Actors Art,

a y n i t ʒ   ʃ ʒ p t
Can dye, and liue, to acte a ʃecond part.

a h a x o   o a t
That's but an Exit of Mortalitie;

T a   e r c a l
This, a Re-entrance to a Plaudite.

I. M.

N⁰ 2.-COMPARISON WITH TYPICAL LETTER OF SAME FORM.

"I.M." POEM.

t m o e M   h e e e

To the memorie of M. *W. Shake-ſpeare.*

E n e   h e e e   a h w t   o o

VVEE wondred (Shake-ſpeare) that thou went'ſt ſo ſoone

F m e   r's a t h   n e   y n a e

From the Worlds-Stage, to the Graues-Tyring-roome.

e a h h d d   t i s y l e   a h

Wee thought thee dead, but this thy printed worth,

l h   p a r h t n   b f t

Tels thy Spectators, that thou went'ſt but forth

o t w h p y   A d's t

To enter with applauſe. An Actors Art,

n e d u o   e e n   a

Can dye, and liue, to acte a ſecond part.

T t u n   i ſ r l i

That's but an Exit of Mortalitie;

h   R n a e a   a

This, a Re-entrance to a Plaudite.

I M

Nº 3 · COMPARISON WITH TYPICAL LETTER OF SAME FORM.

"I.M".POEM.

T h e r o   W a f a

To the memorie of M. W .Shake-fpeare.

w d d   a f a t t o e f t f n

VVEE wondred (Shake-fpeare) that thou went'ft fo foone

r t W l ' S g o e   a s r g o

From the Worlds-Stage, to the Graues-Tyring-roome.

W t u t e e   b t t p n d r

Wee thought thee dead, but this thy printed worth,

T s y e t s a h w t   u o h

Tels thy Spectators, that thou went'ft but forth

e e i a l f   n o A

To enter with applaufe. An Actors Art,

C d a l e   a a c d y

Can dye, and liue, to acte a fecond part.

b ' s t   t M t i e

That's but an Exit of Mortalitie;

i s   e t n t P.

This, a Re-entrance to a Plaudite.

I. M.

N°4-CONTRAST WITH TYPICAL LETTER OF OPPOSITE FORM.

"I.M." POEM.

¹o e ¹⁸m i   ¹⁹S   ²⁰r

To the memorie of M. W. Shake-ſpeare.

²¹E o r ²²S ²³k ^{30·24}p r h t u n ſ o e

VVEE wondred (Shake-ſpeare) that thou went'ſt ſo ſoone

o h o d t e t ²⁵G u ¹⁰T i r ²⁶m

From the Worlds-Stage, to the Graues-Tyring-roome.

e h g t e a y h h r t w t

Wee thought thee dead, but this thy printed worth,

e t 'S & o t t o e ⁸ſt r

Tels thy Spectators, that thou went'ſt but forth

¹⁰T n r t p a e   A r r

To enter with applauſe. An Actors Art,

a ¹¹y n i t & ſ o p t

Can dye, and liue, to acte a ſecond part.

a b a   o o a t

That's but an Exit of Mortalitie;

¹⁰T a e r c o l

This, a Re-entrance to a Plaudite.   I. M.

N°5·CONTRAST WITH TYPICAL LETTER OF OPPOSITE FORM.

"I.M."POEM.

t m o e   h e e e

To the memorie of M. *W*. *Shake-fpeare*.

/   /   /   /   /   /

E n e   h e e e   a h w t o o

VV*EE wondred (Shake-fpeare) that thou went'ft fo foone*

F m e   r s a t h   r e   y n o e

From the Worlds=Stage, to the Graues-Tyring-roome,

/ / /   /   / /   /   / /   / / /

e o h h d t i s y i e o h

Wee thought thee dead, but this thy printed worth,

/   / / /   / /   /   / / / /

l h p a r h t u n b f t

Tels thy Spectators, that thou went'ft but forth

/   / / /   / /   / / /   //   //

o t w h p u A a s t

To enter with applaufe. An Actors Art,

/   / / /   /   /   / /   /

n e u o e n a

Can dye, and liue, to acte a fecond part.

/ / / /   / /   / /   /   //

T t u n i f r t i

That's but an Exit of Mortalitie;

/   / / / / /   / / /

b   R n a e a a

This, a Re-entrance to a Plaudite.

/   / / /   / /   / //

Nº6-CONTRAST WITH TYPICAL LETTER OF OPPOSITE FORM.

"I.M." POEM.

VV

M eee f h i mm ooo r t T

E S aaeeehikpr∫tx   S. W aa eee h k pr ∫

AAA CEE FG M P R SS TTTTT WW

aaaaadaaaaaaaaaas ada bb b cc ddddddd ddd

eeeeeeeeeeeeeeeeee eeeeeeee f∫∫ gg g hhhhhhhhh hhhhhhhh

iiiiiii i llll ll mm nnnnnnn nnnnnnn ooooooooooooo ooooooo

pppp p rrrrr rrrrrrrrrr sssss s ∫∫∫ ∫

ttttttttttttttttttt ttttttttttttttttt

uuuu uuuuuu ww www yyyy

ætætæt is is ∫t ∫t

LETTERS ARRANGED ALPHABETICALLY, CLASSIFIED ACCORDING
TO FORM, AND IN PRINTED ORDER.

"I.M." POEM.

VV

M eee f h i mm ooo r t T

F S aaeeehikprſtx   S W aa eee h k p ſ ſ

AAA C E E F G M P R SS T T T T T ww

aaaaaaaaaaaaaaaaaaa a bbb cc ddddddddd

eeeeeeeeeeeeeeeeeeeeeeeeeeeeee ff g g hhhhhhhhhhhhhhhhhh

iiiiiii llllll mm nnnnnnnnnnnnnnn ooooooooooooooooooooooooo

ppppp rrrrrrrrrrrrrrrr sssss ſſſſ

ttttttttttttttttttttttttttttttttttttt

uuuuuuuuuu wwwww yyyy

ﬄ ﬄ isis ſt ſt

LETTERS ARRANGED ALPHABETICALLY AND IN PRINTED ORDER.

ELIZABETH WELLS GALLUP TESTED AS A DECIPHERER

BY JAMES PHINNEY BAXTER

To the memorie of M. *W. Shake-speare.*

VVEE *wondred* (Shake-speare) *that thou went'st so soone*
From the Worlds-Stage, to the Graues-Tyring-roome.
Wee thought thee dead, but this thy printed worth,
Tels thy Spectators, that thou went'st but forth
To enter with applause. An Actors Art,
Can dye, and liue, to acte a second part.
That's but an Exit of Mortalitie ;
This, a Re-entrance to a Plaudite.

I. M.

To the memorie of M. *W. Shake-speare.*

VVEE *wondred* (Shake-speare) *that thou went'st so soone*
From the Worlds-Stage, to the Graues-Tyring-roome.
Wee thought thee dead, but this thy printed worth,
Tels thy Spectators, that thou went'st but forth
To enter with applause. An Actors Art,
Can dye, and liue, to acte a second part.
That's but an Exit of Mortalitie ;
This, a Re-entrance to a Plaudite.

I. M.

ORIGINAL ARRANGEMENT, I.M. POEM
Shakespeare Folio, 1623
As deciphered by Elizabeth Wells Gallup

```
Tothe memor ieofM WShak espea reWEE wondr
baaab aabaa aaaaa baaaa aaaba aabbb aabab

edSha kespe areth attho uwent stsos ooneF
abbab baaaa abaab aabaa babba aabaa baaab

romth eWorl dsSta getot heGra uesTy ringr
baaba aabbb aabaa aabbb aabaa aaaaa aaabb

oomeW eetho ughtt heede adbut thist hypri
abaaa abbaa aabba baaab abbab aabab baaba

ntedw orthT elsth ySpec tator sthat thouw
aabbb aabaa aaaba abbab aabab aabaa aaabb

entst butfo rthTo enter witha pplau seAnA
abaaa aabaa baaab aabab baaaa aaaaa abbaa

ctors ArtCa ndyea ndliu etoac tease oondp
aaaba abaaa baaab aaaab aaaaa baaaa abbab

artTh atsbu tanEx itofM ortal itieT hisaR
abbaa abbab aabab baabb aabaa baaaa baabb

eentr ancet oaPla udite
ababa aaaaa ababb
```

Search for keyes, the headings of the Comedies.

FRANCIS BARON OF VERULAM.

TEST GIVEN ELIZABETH WELLS GALLUP
By Re-arrangement of Letters, I.M. Poem
Shakespeare Folio 1623

```
Tothe memor ieofM WShak espea reWEE wondr
baaab aabaa aaaaa baaaa aaaba aabbb abaab

edSha kespe areth attho uwent stsos ooneF
aaaaa abaaa baaab aabaa baaaa abaab baabb

romth eWorl dsSta getot heGra uesTy ringr
ababa baaba baabb baaaa abaab baaaa abaaa

oomeW eetho ughtt heede adbut thist hypri
aabaa aabba baabb abbaa aaabb baaab aaaba

ntedw orthT elsth ySpec tator sthat thouw
aabbb ababa aaaaa aaaba aabbb baaba aabaa

entst butfo rthTo enter witha pplau seAnA
abbaa ababb aaaaa aaaba aabbb baaba abaaa

ctors ArtCa ndyea ndliu etoac tease condp
baaab baaba baaaa aabaa aaaba aabbb baaba

artTh atsbu tanEx itofM ortal itieT hisaR
abbaa abbab aabab baabb aabaa baaaa baabb

eentr ancet oaPla udite
ababa aaaaa ababb
```

Search Kaiser Kultur Krieg und Schlachten
Macht ist Recht n of Verulam.

It is hoped that the presentation of the Bi-literal Cipher in the preceding pages, showing its existence in the pages of the 1623 Folio Edition, and of the manner of its decipherment, will not be confused with the discredited "discovery" by Ignatius Donnelly—page 26. Donnelly endeavored to follow the directions laid down by Bacon in applying the Bi-literal Cipher, but he failed to carry out the very principles he gathered—and hence his failure. The strength of the Bi-literal Cipher lies in the fact that it is Bacon's own. The discovery of the application consists only in the skill and patience which carrying out his directions necessitates.

That the Bi-literal Cipher is only one of many found in 16th and 17th Century Literature, is attested by page 27. Here are enumerated six ciphers, descriptions of which have been brought to light through the Bi-literal Cipher. In this connection, the reader will remember Bacon's own statement and enumeration on page 6 of various kinds and forms of ciphers.

WHERE IGNATIUS DONNELLEY FELL DOWN ON THE CIPHER.
He failed to note the difference in the bi-form
character of type, and missed the application.

Then take your interior epistle, reduced to the biliteral shape, and adapt to it letter by letter your exterior epistle in the biform character; and then write it out. Let the exterior epistle be:

DO NOT GO TILL I COME.

Example of adaptation.

F   L   Y

aa bab ab abab a   bba

Do not go   till· I come.

I add another large example of the same cipher — of the writing of anything by anything.

The interior epistle, for which I have selected the Spartan dispatch, formerly sent in the *Scytale :*

All is lost. Mindarus is killed. The soldiers want food. We can neither get hence nor stay longer here.

The exterior epistle, taken from Cicero's first letter and containing the Spartan dispatch within it:

In all duty or rather piety towards you I satisfy everybody except myself. Myself I never satisfy. For so great are the services which you have rendered me, that, seeing you did not rest in your endeavors on my behalf till the thing was done, I feel as if my life had lost ALL *its sweetness, because I cannot do as much in this cause of yours. The occasions are these: Ammonius the king's ambassador openly besieges us with money, the business* IS *carried on through the same creditors who were employed in it when you were here,* etc.

I have here capitalized the words *all* and *is,* supposing them to be part of the sentence, "All is lost," but I am not sure that I am right in doing so. The sentence ends as above and leaves us in the dark. Bacon·continues:

This doctrine of ciphers carries along with it another doctrine which is its relative. This is the doctrine of deciphering, or of detecting ciphers, though one be quite ignorant of the alphabet used or the private understanding between the parties: a thing requiring both labor and ingenuity, and dedicated, as the other likewise is, to the secrets of princes: By skillful precaution indeed it may be made useless; though, as things are, it is of very great use. For if good and safe ciphers were introduced, there are very many of them which altogether elude and exclude the decipherer, and yet are sufficiently convenient and ready to read and write. But such is the rawness and unskillfulness of secretaries and clerks in the courts of kings, that the greatest matters are commonly trusted to weak and futile ciphers.

I said to myself: What is there unreasonable in the thought that this man, who dwelt with such interest upon the subject of ciphers, who had invented ciphers, even ciphers within ciphers — that this subtle and most laborious intellect might have injected a cipher narrative, an "interior epistle," into the Shakespeare Plays, in which he would assert his authorship of the same, and reclaim for all time those "children of his brain" who had been placed, for good and sufficient reasons, under the fosterage of another?

I. Bi-Literal Cipher.

A	B	C	D	E	F
aaaaa	aaaab	aaaba	aaabb	aabaa	aabab
11111	11112	11121	11122	11211	11212
-----	----/	---/-	---//	--/--	--/-/
G	H	I	K	L	M
aabba	aabbb	abaaa	abaab	ababa	ababb
11221	11222	12111	12112	12121	12122
--//-	--///	-/---	-/--/	-/-/-	-/-//
N	O	P	Q	R	S
abbaa	abbab	abbba	abbbb	baaaa	baaab
12211	12212	12221	12222	21111	21112
-//--	-//-/	-///-	-////	/----	/---/
T	U	W	X	Y	Z
baaba	baabb	babaa	babab	babba	babbb
21121	21122	21211	21212	21221	21222
/--/-	/--//	/-/--	/-/-/	/-//-	/-///

The alphabet which is called the key of this cipher was first represented by combinations of a and b, in groups of five. Anything capable of two differences may represent the key, as figures, or other characters in writing; lights, bells, flags, etc. in signaling. An example of the key is given in three forms. It is clear that in order to employ such an alphabet in writing or in printing, one must have both capital and small letters in two forms to represent the a and the b, or 1 and 2 or - / of the key alphabet. It will also be seen that each cipher letter requires five written or printed letters, therefore the finished work will contain at least five times the number of letters as the cipher epistle. This is what is meant by the quintuple proportion of one to the other.

II. Anagram Cipher

A cipher in which by the transposition of the letters of words, phrases or sentences, other words or statements may be made. A good example is the long word in Love's Labour's Lost, p. 136.

III. Capital Letter Cipher

A cipher in which capital letters in two forms carry a secret message.

IV. Clock or Time Cipher

A cipher in which the numbers from 1 to 12 are keys. The numbers indicate how many words stand between the key and the word to be taken.

V. Symbol Cipher

A cipher in which certain symbols have a definite meaning assigned by the writer. It was chiefly used to point out other ciphers.

VI. Word Cipher

A cipher in which guide words indicate works; key words mark certain portions, and joining words show which parts are to be brought together. The first two of these are usually given in an auxiliary cipher.

A Form

B Form

The typical letter is plain with high, straight bar. A kern or a dot in the letter changes it from a to b or vice versa.

The typical letter is plain with a curved or slanting bar, as seen in the alphabet.

A long letter extending below the line.

No example.

No example.

Top and bottom lines parallel; the kern on the base line slender and slanting.

No example

Top heavy and slants parallel to seriph of base.

No example.

The short line slants toward the base.

No example

Kern short, straight, and blunt at the right. Third line shaded from top. Seriphs at bottom level.

Has a nearly even curve in the top at the right.

No example,

No example

Top forms a segment of a circle at the left. Upright does not reach the top.

No example

Erect; round curves.

Curved top.

No example.

A tall, well-made letter,

The heavy, blunt letter with short connecting line is the b-form. It is accented and therefore marked a-form.

No example

Large size type, narrow head and wide base.

No example

Well-made letter in large size type ; points sharp.

LARGE LOWER CASE ITALIC LETTERS IN
"THE I·M· POEM"

<u>A Form</u>		<u>B Form</u>

Slanting, somewhat wide at the base.

 a

No example.

If the end of the curve of the base line were produced it would not form a perfect <u>o</u>.

 e

If the end of the curve of the base line were produced it would form a perfect <u>o</u>.

Somewhat slender; the loop is narrow at the top and pointed.

 h

No example.

Slender and delicate; the queue not widely spread at base.

 k

No example.

The loop is narrow in the bottom part.

 p

No example.

Somewhat broad at the top; both kerns are rounded.

 r

No example.

Long, well-made letter; the stem is a wave line.

No example.

A Form

a

B Form

Typical a form is well-made;
the oval usually shows angle or
shoulder and rounds gradually to
the line of writing, making the
letter somewhat wider at the base
than the corresponding letter in
the b form; also the oval has the
appearance of a complete o placed
in such a way that a part of one side
side rests on the upright and often
projects sufficiently to give the
stem the appearance of bending
outward near the center.

Somewhat narrower at base
than the a form; oval pointed;
upright is often either uniform
or slightly heavier at top.
Letter slanted.

Oval pointed at top and
narrow at base.

Oval rounded at top; upright
straight nearly to the base.

Roundness commences near
top; curve at base usually wide.

Roundness commences near
center of back; curve at base
usually narrow.

Stem has no wave line, but
sometimes turns slightly to the
left at top; toe upturned; loop
leaves stem and rejoins it at a
somewhat obtuse angle.

Wave line in stem, angle
between stem and top of oval acute;
point of jointure below, somewhat
high on stem.

A line drawn through the
loop of this letter beginning at
the left of the oval where it leaves
the stem and running through the
opposite point of the oval, in-
tersects the line of the end of
the curve of the base produced
either above or below the line
of writing.

A line drawn through the
loop of this letter beginning
at the left of the oval where it
leaves the stem and running
through the opposite point of
the oval, will run parallel to the
line of the end of the curve of
the base produced.

Letter slanted; straight top,
or, if curved, showing a small neck
at left.

Letter stands nearly erect;
top curved.

<u>A Form</u>

<u>B Form</u>

g

The lower loop is attached to the center of the oval; the connecting line usually heavy and angular.

The lower loop is attached a little to the left of the center of the oval; the connecting line is usually thin.

h

The stem of this letter is not characteristic, unless perhaps slightly pointed at the base; a line drawn upward through the loop so as to intersect it at the middle of the upper part of the curve tends only slightly toward the right.

The stem of the letter is characteristic; a line drawn upward through the loop so as to intersect it at the middle of the upper part of the curve tends pronouncedly toward the right.

In the typical letter of this class the base is usually rounded; the kerns do not correspond, that is, one will be straight and the other curved.

In the typical letter of this class the kerns at the ends, whether curved or straight show a correspondence with each other.

The typical letter of this class usually shows a slight wave line in the stem. The angle made by the kern and the stem is large.
Double letters are governed by the law of digraphs, not by that of single letters.

The typical letter of this class has the characteristic stem rounded into a small, close kern.

m

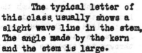

The second loop shorter at top and turns slightly to the right; width of loops nearly equal at base; top kern inclined to sharpness; kern at base usually close.

Nearly even at top; second loop wider at base than the first; top kern rounded, and corresponds to the kern at the base.

A Form

Letter slanting; top kern inclined to sharpness; kern at base usually clear. The loop tends toward the right at the top in the same manner as that of the second loop in the <u>a</u> form of <u>m</u>

There are many varieties of small <u>o</u>, and it is difficult to assign them to their proper classes. The <u>a</u> form letters show the slant characteristic of that form and are best classified by comparing them with the capital letter, which is less symmetrical than the <u>b</u> form.

Stem of nearly uniform thickness throughout, or slightly shaded below the line of writing; loop shows only slight narrowing toward the base, but slants downward where joined to the upright.

The letter has the slant that is characteristic of the <u>a</u> form. The first kern is small and tends to sharpness; the second kern is rounded. There is usually a greater breadth at the top in the <u>a</u> form than in the <u>b</u> form.

There are long and short letters in both forms. The base in either case is nearly horizontal. The long <u>s</u> of the <u>a</u> form is more slanting than that of the <u>b</u> form.

B Form

Nearly erect; top kern usually rounded; the two kerns correspond. The letter shows a wideness at the base corresponding to that of the second loop in the <u>b</u> form of <u>m</u>.

If a line were drawn lightly along the inside of the capital <u>O</u> of the <u>b</u> form it would show almost perfect symmetry. This appears also in all the well-printed lower-case letters of this form.

Stem often thick at top; loop joins the upright almost at a right angle.

The left kern is usually distinct and strong; the two differ only slightly. The upward stroke of the letter is usually strong and distinct. The letter is usually somewhat narrow at the top.

The long <u>s</u> of the <u>b</u> form is usually upturned at the base and the slant of the letter is not marked. The short letter has the same characteristics.

LOWER CASE ITALIC LETTERS IN
"THE I.M. POEM"

a Form		b Form

a Form

Stem of nearly uniform thickness, turns slightly to the right a little above the base.

b Form

Stem usually heavy at the top, diminishes gradually toward the base; foot free.

The typical letter of this class has the slant of the a-form; the first kern straight; the second curved, or <u>vice versa</u>. The connecting line between the uprights is lower than in the b-form.

Letter nearly erect; the kerns correspond with each other. The connecting line joins the second upright at a higher point in the b-form than in the a-form.

First point of base sharp, second point blunt. The letter is flat topped.

Both points of base sharp; first and third stroke on the left extend in curves above the level of the body of the letter.

Narrow at top; second stroke bends toward the first.

No example.

DESCRIPTION OF THE DIGRAPHS IN
"THE I. M. POEM".

The union of a slanting c
that shows an angle in the base,
with a t that comes well down to
the line of writing with the
slant of the a form, gives the
combination "aa".

No example.

The union of a slanting c
that shows an angle in the base,
with a t that approaches the c at
the base, and has a cross-bar that
thickens toward the right gives the
combination "ab".

The union of c well-rounded
at the base with a t that comes
well down to the line of writing
with the slant of the a form,
gives the combination "ba".

The union of a short, well-
rounded i with an s narrow in the
head and angular in the base gives
the combination "aa".

No example.

No example.

The union of a somewhat
large i, the kern and base
corresponding, with an s
narrow in the head gives the
combination "ba".

The union of a long s
having a wide curve at the top,
with a t having a slanting bar
and somewhat wide angle between
the foot and the stem gives the
combination "aa".

No example.

ROMAN TYPE IN TITLE
Upper Case

a Form	b Form

M

Large and heavy. There
is no kern at the top of the
second upright.

No example

T

A plain, simple letter, with
the top and the seriph parallel,
the former usually a thin line.
—P.A. & CAT.

Usually heavier than the
a-form. The top shades somewhat heavily into the kerns,
and is not parallel to the seriph
at the base.

Lower Case

e

The letter is wide, slender,
the bar horizontal.

Somewhat heavier than the
a-form usually; well-rounded;
the bar slightly slanting.

f

A well-made letter, the
curve at the top somewhat wide.

No example

h

The letter is somewhat heavy,
and is wide at the top of the
loop.

The letter is somewhat more
delicate than the a-form and
is wide at the base. P.A.

i

The kern is sharp and prominent, giving the letter an
unnatural appearance.

Well-made and regular, but
somewhat heavy. — P.A. & Cat.

ROMAN TYPE IN TITLE
Lower Case

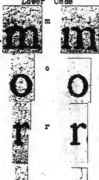

<u>a Form</u>

The first curve at the top leaves the stem at a high point.

Slightly irregular in outline.

Wide at the top; well-made.

There are several variants but all curve upward at base and are somewhat narrow.

<u>b Form</u>

The curves are regular; the seriphs at the base slant downward in a regular succession.

The letter is tall and somewhat heavy, but well-made. P.A.

Narrow; not particularly well-formed. — P.A. & Cat.

The letter is very wide and flat at the base. — P.A.

ROMAN TYPE IN POEM
Upper Case

<u>A Form</u>

Top and Base not horizontal.

The curves of nearly equal width. — Dig.

Lower Case

A broad, well-made letter; the stem rounds into a free foot.

Somewhat irregular; the lower part is often narrow.

The loop has a shallow curve at the top, and is somewhat wide.

<u>B Form</u>

No example

The curves are somewhat wide; the top narrower than the base; the letter symmetrical.

The stem bends slightly to the left at the base and the foot turns sharply upward.

A well-made letter with a light bar. — Pro.

The loop leaves the stem with a clear curve; the right seriph is low at the base.— Dig.

a Form		b Form

a Form

Somewhat delicate and well-made; the stem is narrow at the top and widens slightly at the base. — Dig. & Pro.

b Form

Heavy; of nearly uniform thickness throughout; the upper kern prominent.

Broad and well-made although somewhat heavy.— Dig.

Somewhat slender and delicate; seriphs carefully placed.

Broad; the loop is somewhat flat at the top.

A delicate letter with the loop well rounded top and bottom. Where it occurs it is changed by a dot to the a-form. — Dig.

The top shows a line at the right turning somewhat abruptly downwards. —Pro. & Dig.

The upward stroke at the right and its downward curve correspond in slope and direction as would the two sides of an isosceles triangle.

Long form with wide top and shallow curve.

Short curve at the top and somewhat slender stem.— Dig.

The letter has a wide top and a wide base that becomes nearly horizontal.

The base of this form turns soon after leaving the stem.— Dig.

No example

A tall, somewhat awkward letter, wider at top than at the base.

To the memorie of M. W. Shake-speare.

VVEE wondred (Shake-speare) that thou went'st so soone
From the Worlds-Stage, to the Graues-Tyring-roome.
Wee thought thee dead, but this thy printed worth,
Tels thy Spectators, that thou went'st but forth
To enter with applause. An Actors Art,
Can dye, and liue, to acte a second part.
That's but an Exit of Mortalitie;
This, a Re-entrance to a Plaudite.

I. M.

To the memorie of M. W. Shake-speare.

VVEE wondred (Shake-speare) that thou went'st so soone
From the Worlds-Stage, to the Graues-Tyring-roome.
Wee thought thee dead, but this thy printed worth,
Tels thy Spectators, that thou went'st but forth
To enter with applause. An Actors Art,
Can dye, and liue, to acte a second part.
That's but an Exit of Mortalitie;
This, a Re-entrance to a Plaudite.

I. M.

SHAKESPEARE FOLIO 1623—METHUEN COPY

ALPHABET

A-aaaaa
B-aaaab
C-aaaba
D-aaabb
E-aabaa
F-aabab
G-aabba
H-aabbb
I-abaaa
K-abaab
L-ababa
M-ababb
N-abbaa
O-abbab
P-abbba
Q-abbbb
R-baaaa
S-baaab
T-baaba
V-baabb
W-babaa
X-babab
Y-babba
Z-babbb

I. M. POEM

```
To the memor  icef'l  dShak  espee  re EE  wondr  edsha  kespe  areth  atths  twent  stees  esneF
baaab  aabaa  aaaaa  baaaa  aaaba  aabbb  aabab  abbab  baaaa  abaab  aabaa  babba  aabaa  baaab

remth  eWerl  deSta  getet  heGra  uesTy  ringr  semeY  eethe  ughtt  heede  adbut  thist  hypri
baaba  aabbb  aabaa  aabbb  aabaa  aaaaa  aaabb  abaaa  abbaa  aabba  baaab  abbab  aabab  baaba

ntedw  erthT  elsih  ySpec  tater  sthat  theuw  entst  butfe  rthTe  enter  witha  pplau  seAmA
aabbb  aabaa  aaaba  abbab  ababb  aabaa  aaabb  abaaa  aabaa  baaab  aabab  baaaa  aaaaa  abbaa

cters  ArtCa  ndyea  ndliu  eteac  tease  condp  artTh  atpbu  tanEx  itefM  ertal  itieT  hiaaR
aaaba  abaaa  baaab  aaaab  aaaaa  baraa  abbaa  abbaa  abbab  aabab  baabb  aabaa  baaaa  baabb

centr  ancet  eaPla  udite  IM
ababa  aaaaa  ababb
```

Search for keyes, the headings of the Comedies.

FRANCIS BARON OF VERULAM.

TYPICAL LETTERS IN "I.M." POEM.
Italic (Case 2)

Letter		a Form Line	Word	Letter		b Form Line	Word
A		5	Art	A		5	An
C		6	Can	C	Cat.	5	Comedy
E	Pro.	20	Expectation	E		1	WEE
F	Dig.	7	Fresh	F		2	From
G	Pro.	1	Greece	G		2	Graues
M	Dig.	4	Moniment	M		7	Mortalitie
P		8	Plaudite	P	Pro.	7 ·	Put
R	Pro.	6	Regall	R		8	Re-entrance
S	Dig.	18	Sword	S		4	Spectators
T		2	Tyring	T	Pro.	15	Their
W		3	Wee	W		2	Worlds (dotted to make "a")

Italic (Case 1)

Letter		a Form Line	Word	Letter		b Form Line	Word
a		5	applause	a		4	Spectators
b		4	but	b		3	but
c		8	Re-entrance	c	Dig.	2	which
d		6	second	d		3	printed
e		1	wondred	e		1	went'st
f		4	forth	f		7	of
g		2	Stage	g		2	Tyring
h		5	with	h		3	thy
i		3	printed	i		7	Mortalitie
l		6	liue	l		2	Worlds
m		2	From	m	Dig.	3	must
n		5	enter	n		7	an
o		3	worth	o		2	Worlds
p		3	printed	p		4	Spectators
r		2	Graues	r		4	forth
ſ		6	ſecond	ſ		1	ſo
s		2	Worlds	s		7	That's
t		1	that	t		4	thy
u		3	but	u		1	thou
w		1	wondred	w		5	with
y		4	thy	y	Dig.	2	thy (2nd)

TYPICAL LETTERS IN "I.M." POEM.

Italic (Case 3)

a form			b form		
Letter	Line	Word	Letter	Line	Word
a	Title	Shakespeare	a	P.A. 1 R	Samuel
e	"	Shakespeare	e	Title	Shakespeare
h	"	Shakespeare	h	P.A. 6 R	Nicholas
k		Shakespeare	k	—	—
p		Shakespeare	p	—	—
r		Shakespeare	r	P.A. 2 L	Richard
ſ		Shakeſpeare	ſ	P.A. 8 R	Joſeph

Italic (Case 4)

a Form			b Form		
Letter	Line	Word	Letter	Line	Word
S	Title	Shakespeare	S	P.A. 1 L	Shakespeare
W	P.A. 5 L	William	W	Title 1	W

Large Roman (Case 7)

a Form			b Form		
Letter	Line	Word	Letter	Line	Word
e	Title	memorie	e	Title	the
f	"	of	f	—	—
h	"	the	h	P.A. Tit. 6	these
i	"	memorie	i	P.A. " 3	Tragedies
m	"	memorie	m	Title	memorie
o		To	o	Cat. Tit. 3	Volume
r	"	memorie	r	P.A. " 3	Tragedies
t		the	t	P.A. " 3	set

Large Roman.(Case 8)

a Form			b Form		
Letter	Line	Word	Letter	Line	Word
M	Title	M	M		——
T	Cat. Sub-Title	HISTORIES	T	Title	To

	a Form				b Form	
Letter	Line	Word	Letter		Line	Word
a	1	Shakespeare	a		1	Shakespeare
e	1	Shakespeare	e	Dig.	16	Iuliet
h	1	Shakespeare	h	Dig.	9	Shakespeares
i	Dig. 16	Iuliet	i		7	Exit
k	Dig. 1	SHakespeare	k		1	Shakespeare
p	1	Shakespeare	p	Dig.	1	SHakespeare
r	Dig. 9	Shakespeares	r		1	Shakespeare
ſ	1	Shakeſpeare	ſ	Dig.	9	Shakeſpeares
t	7	Exit	t	Dig.	4	Stratford
x	----------		x		7	Exit

Small Roman (Case 6)

	a Form			b Form	
Letter	Line	Word	Letter	Line	Word
E	7	Exit	E		--------
S	Dig. 21	Shakespeare	S.	1	Shakespeare

Initial Large Roman (Case 10) W--b form

Italic (Case 1)
Digraphs.

Digraph	Line	Word	Digraph		Line	Word
ct	5	Actors	is	Dig.	3	is
ct	6	acte	ſt		1	wentʃt
ct	4	Spectators	ſt	Dig.	3	muſt
ct	Pro. 20	Expectation	ſt	Dig.	3	ſtone
is	8	This	ſt	Dig. 14	miſt
is	Dig. 5	This			
is	3	this			

DOTTED LETTERS

Letters which are changed to the opposite form because of the presence of one or three dots are indicated in the photographs of the alphabets by a large dot above the letter.

"I.M." POEM

Line	Word	Letter	Form	changed to
1	soone	e	b	a
2	the (1st)	h	b	a
2	Worlds	W	b	a
3	thought		b	a
3	thee		b	a
3	printed	^	a	b
4	thou		b	a
4	forth	h	b	a
5	enter		b	a
5	applause		b	a
6	and		b	a
6	liue	u	a	b
6	part	p	a	b
8	a (1st)	a	a	b
8	a (2nd)	a	a	b
Title	of		b	a

"I.M." POEM

Reference numbers to letters taken from other places.

Letter	Case	Form	From	Line	Word
o	7	b	Cat.	Tit. 3	Volume
T	8	a	Cat.	Sub-title	HISTORIES
r	7	b	P.A.	Tit. 3	Tragedies
W	4	a	P.A.	5 L	William
'a	3	b	P.A.	1 R	Samuel
ſſ	5	b	P.A.	8 R	Joſeph
ſſ	5	b	Dig.	9	Shakeſpeares
ſR	1	bb	Dig.	14	miſt
S	2	a	Pro.	1	Scene
T	2	b	Pro.	15	Their
y	1	b	Dig.	2	thy (2nd)
C	2	b	Cat.	5	Comedy
c	1	b	Dig.	2	which
t	5	b	Dig.	4	Stratford
M	2	a	Dig.	4	Moniment
is	1	bb	Dig.	3	is
P	2	b	Pro.	7	Put
i	7	b	P.A.	Tit. 3	according
S	4	b	P.A.	1 L	Shakespeare
r	3	b	P.A.	2 L	Richard
E	2	a	Pro.	20	Expectation
S	6	a	Dig.	21	Shakespeare
k	5	a	Dig.	1	SHakespeare
r	5	a	Dig.	9	Shakespeares
G	2	a	Pro.	1	Greece
m	1	b	Dig.	3	must
h	3	b	P.A.	6 R	Nicholas
h	5	b	Dig.	9	Shakespeares
e	5	b	Dig.	16	Iuliet
F	2	a	Dig.	7	Freſh
is	1	ab	Dig.	5	This
ct	1	bb	Pro.	20	Expectation
i	5	a	Dig.	16	Iuliet
R	2	a	Pro.	6	Regall
ſt	1	ab	Dig.	3	muſt
ſt	1	ba	Dig.	3	ſtone
h	7	b	P.A.	Tit. 6	these
t	7	b	P.A.	3	set
p	5	b	Dig.	1	SHakespeare (dotted)

THE CATALOGVE

of the several Comedies, Histories, and Tragedies contained in the Cipher

COMEDIES

Seven Wise Men of the West

Solomon the Second

The Mouse Trap

HISTORIES

The Life of Elizabeth

The Life of the Earl of Essex

The White Rose of Britain

The Life and Death of Edward the
Third

The Life of Henry the Seventh

TRAGEDIES

Mary Queen of Scots

Robert, the Earl of Essex (my late
brother)

Robert, the Earl of Leicester (my late
father)

The Life and Death of Christopher
Marlowe

Anne Bullen

NOTABLE TRANSLATIONS

The Iliad   (Homer)

The Odyssey   (Homer)

The Æneid   (Virgil)

The Eclogues, and a few short
    poems   (Virgil)

MISCELLANEOUS

The Life of Robert Greene

Two Secret Epistles, expressly teaching a Cipher

Completion of the New Atlantis

A Pastoral of the Christ

Bacchantes, a fantasy

History, in prose commixed with
    verse, of England and a few
    Englishmen.

Story in verse of the Spanish Armada.

Bacon's own story of his life, in which
    Marguerite de Valois figures.

A number of short poems in French,
    written for Marguerite, form a
    part of the story of Bacon's life
    in France.

THESE TITLES ARE FROM WORKS PUBLISHED IN THE XVITH AND XVIITH CENTURIES,
DECIPHERED BY ELIZABETH WELLS GALLUP

A CATALOGVE

of the ſeuerall Comedies, Hiſtories, and Tragedies contained in this Volume.